Pacific Halibut
Flat or Fiction?

Written by Lauri Sadorus

Illustrated by Birgit Soderlund

International Pacific Halibut Commission

Established by a convention between
Canada and the United States of America

Commissioners

Clifford Atleo	James Balsiger
Richard Beamish	Ralph Hoard
Phillip Lestenkof	Gary Robinson

Director
Bruce M. Leaman

International Pacific Halibut Commission
2320 W Commodore Way, Suite 300
Seattle, WA 98199-1287
www.iphc.int
First Printing 2005

ISBN 0-9776931-0-4

Flat or Fiction?

What would you say if I told you that there is a fish at the bottom of the Pacific Ocean that can grow to be as long as a car, and can weigh as much as 10 first graders?

Let me tell you about Pacific halibut!

 Look for this glossary symbol on the pages ahead, then find out what the words mean on page 23.

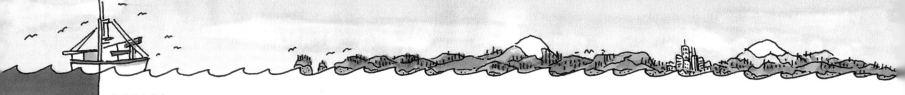

What Do Halibut Look Like?

Pacific halibut are in the flounder family. Their scientific name is *Hippoglossus stenolepis*. Hippo-gloss-us, means "horse tongue", and refers to a halibut's large mouth and tongue. Sten-o-lep-is means "narrow scale" and refers to the deeply embedded, almost invisible scales on the halibut's body.

Flat Fact!
A layer of slime that feels a little like dish washing liquid covers a halibut's whole body. The slime is important to keep infection out.

Like all flounders, halibut are flat and spend most of their lives on the ocean floor. Don't let "flat" fool you though. While halibut may be only as thick as a book, they can reach weights of 500 pounds or more!

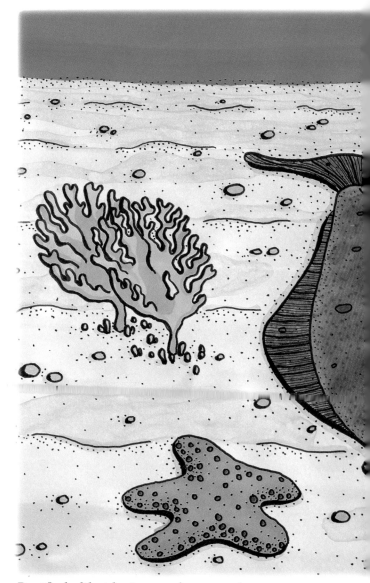

Pacific halibut laying on the ocean bottom.

4

How do halibut protect themselves from predators?

The ocean is full of many different kinds of animals. Although halibut can grow pretty big and are hearty swimmers, there is sometimes a bigger animal waiting in the depths. As it turns out, protection for halibut comes by hiding — in plain sight!

Shark - a predator of halibut

Halibut nestle into just about any type of ocean bottom such as sand, mud, and rocks. The top of their bodies are brown and green and sometimes a mix of colors to match the color of the different types of ocean floor. By blending into their surroundings (also called camouflage), they are almost invisible to predators.

Ⓖ predator, camouflage

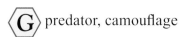

Ask a Simple Question

Sometimes asking a simple question can get you a lot of answers. The more scientists know about halibut, the better the chance of helping to keep the population healthy.

In the ports

One way to gather information is to ask the folks who use halibut. Commission biologists work closely with halibut fishers and plant processors to get an idea of where the fish are caught, how big, and how old they are.

Aboard the survey, scientists collect earbones and other information about halibut such as its length and whether it's male or female.

On the boats

Another way to gain information is to conduct Halibut Commission surveys. Each summer the Commission hires commercial fishing boats and crews to set gear in a specific pattern. Comparing information from one year to the next tells scientists a lot about how fast halibut are growing and the size of the population.

(G) population

Tag, You're It!

Commission scientists have found that one of the best ways to learn about halibut is by tagging them. Tagging is when biologists mark a halibut in some way so it can be identified later, then release it back into the wild.

There are different kinds of tags. Some are put on the outside of the fish. Others are put under their skin, like the tags your dog or cat might get at the vet in case they become lost.

Another kind of tag — called a satellite tag — is about the size of a hotdog and records information about the fish's behavior. This high tech gadget gives researchers a glimpse of what a halibut does morning, noon, and night.

Flat Fact:
Scientists discovered that halibut like to travel when the fish they had tagged in one place showed up hundreds of miles away the next time they were captured.

Satellite tags release from the fish and send information to the Halibut Commission office in much the same way a television show can be broadcast around the world.

Pacific Halibut Are Worth Keeping

What can you do to make sure these magnificent fish are around for a long time?
Taking care of the environment in your home town helps to keep the oceans clean. So, the same things you are probably already doing will also help to keep halibut healthy: conserve water, recycle, ask your parents to use non-toxic cleaners and organic fertilizers whenever possible, and maybe even plant a tree.

Contact us
If you would like to find out more about anything you've read here, please write to:

International Pacific Halibut Commission
2320 W Commodore Way, Suite 300
Seattle, WA 98199-1287
Or visit our website at www.iphc.int

The scientists and commissioners of the International Pacific Halibut Commission hope you have enjoyed this book. When it comes to science - Keep Fishing!

Note to parents and educators
Please feel free to reproduce the last page of this book as desired for creative classroom or at-home projects. Some ideas might be to have students describe (in pictures or words) the halibut life cycle, harvest, habitat, or behavior.

lossary

Camouflage
The colors and markings on an animal that help it blend in with its environment. (kam-oh-flogh)

Continental shelf and slope
The shelf is the shallow, underwater plain that borders the continent. The shelf generally ends in a steep drop-off to the deep ocean floor, called the slope.

Migration
Moving from one place to another.

Otolith
The small bone found in the head of a fish and used to tell how old the fish is. (oh-tow-lith)

Plankton layer
A layer in the ocean where the water has lots of nutrients that help tiny plants called phytoplankton (fy-tow-plank-ton) grow. Tiny shrimp-like animals, called zooplankton (zoe-plank-ton) come to eat the plants, and many small fishes and even some whales eat the zooplankton. It's a busy place.

Population
A word used to describe all the individual halibut as one group.

Predator and Prey
An animal that eats another animal is called the predator. The animal being eaten is called prey.

Spawning
A female halibut lays her eggs and a male halibut then fertilizes them.

Subsistence fishing
Fishing for only the amount needed to feed your family and sometimes others in the community.

Pacific Halibut Flat or Fiction © Copyright 2005